SILHOUETTES OF THE SOUL

Anveyshika Misra

Made with ❤ on the BookLeaf Publishing Platform
www.bookleafpub.in
www.bookleafpub.com

Dedication

To my mother, the guiding light of my soul, whose unwavering belief in the universe's magic shaped my every step.
For all those who trust in the boundless power of the soul, this is for you...

Preface

In your hands lies a collection that seeks to unravel the complexities of life, the mind, and the heart — a journey through realms both seen and unseen, explored and unexplored. This compilation, crafted with sincerity and introspection, is not just for the reader but for the soul that seeks a deeper connection to the universe. With 40 poems, each one paints a unique landscape, inviting you to traverse through varied emotions, ideas, and experiences. From the playful musings of our generation's quirks to the profound depths of spiritual awakening, this book is a reflection of the many facets of the human condition — raw, real, and unapologetically true.

As you turn the pages, be prepared to be swept into an emotional kaleidoscope — one moment you may laugh at the absurdity of modern life, and the next, sit still in the gravity of a deeper truth. These poems span tones and textures — from wit to wonder, confusion to clarity, chaos to calm. They reflect on love, loss, the subconscious mind, the soul's silence, and the cosmic dance of our existence. The poems in this book will resonate in ways that are both familiar and unfamiliar, urging you to dig deeper into your own life and discover the layers of wisdom and wonder that lie within. More than anything, they offer a quiet invitation to pause, feel, and perhaps see yourself more clearly — in a way you hadn't before.

So as you begin reading, let yourself be open to what this collection holds. These aren't just poems — they're tiny mirrors and doorways, waiting to spark something in you. And if, by the end, even one line lingers with you longer than expected... then these words have done what they came here to do.

Acknowledgements

First, I extend my deepest gratitude to my **parents**, whose boundless love and unwavering faith in me have been the foundation of everything I do. To my **mom**, for imparting to me the pious wisdom and invaluable knowledge that has fueled the creation of this collection, and to my **dad**, for his constant encouragement and support, which has empowered me to follow my own path with confidence.

I would also like to thank my **family** for their endless support, love, and blessings, which have been a cornerstone of my growth.

A heartfelt thank you to the **friends**, whose presence and support have been a constant throughout this journey. You have been my pillars, silently cheering me on.

To all the **mentors** and guides — whether through workshops, courses, or life lessons — whose wisdom, intentional or not, has contributed to the essence of this book, thank you.

And finally, **Thank You, Universe**, for always guiding me and making this possible.

INDEX

INDEX

INDEX

INDEX

PART I

5

STIRRING OF THE SOUL

1. Awakening the Infinite Power Within You

In you, the flame of strength resides,
A force unseen, where power hides.
Like Lord Hanuman, who soared through skies,
Within you burns the same surprise.

Forgotten power, untapped and vast,
Lies dormant, waiting to be cast.
A truth so pure, yet deep inside,
Unveiling now, no place to hide.

A leap so great, across the seas,
The universe bends, with gentle ease.
Like Lord Hanuman, with one swift thought,
The world, it bows to what you sought.

In every heartbeat, the stars align,
The cosmos speaks through you, divine.
The soul that sleeps within your chest,
Holds strength unknown, a sacred quest.

Awake, arise, the world awaits,
Beyond the veils of love and fates.
You are the one who moves the tides,
With power deep where truth abides.

The power, like Lord Hanuman's might,
Shines brightest when you claim your light.
No sea too vast, no dream too wide,
Your soul has wings, you must decide.

In every step, the earth will quake,
A force untold, for you to make.
The world is waiting for your rise,
For within you is the vastest prize.

The echoes of the universe roar,
They call to you from every shore.
Awaken now, and feel it true,
The power within, it lies in you.

2. My Mind's Own Party

One quiet night, as I lay in bed,
A thousand guests stormed through my head.
They came uncalled, no invite sent,
But oh, how loud their entrance went.

The worrier wore a wrinkled suit,
Kept pacing round, all anxious and mute.
The dreamer came in floating high,
Dragging stars across the sky.

Regret arrived with perfume past,
Kept showing photos from the last.
While Ego, drunk on pride and fame,
Insisted we all toast his name.

Doubt tapped the walls to check for cracks,
Then whispered secrets at my back.
Hope wore yellow, lit the floor,
And asked me what I'm waiting for.

The shy ones stood near exit signs,
The loud ones spoke in crooked lines.
Overthinking played the DJ set,
And spun remixes of old regret.

Curiosity brought board games in,
While Logic frowned, "We never win."
The creative ones made forts with chairs,
And painted galaxies on all the stairs.

Imagination wore a hat,
That looked like cheese and smelled like cat.
Distraction danced with sheer delight,
And changed the topic every night.

Ambition gave a TEDx talk,
Then left mid-speech to take a walk.
Sarcasm joked with Confidence,
While Puns made zero honest sense.

Procrastination, as always, spilled the tea,
Then promised it was meant to be.
Gratitude brought cookies 'round,
And Self-Love laid a picnic ground.

Peace sat humming soft and low,
While Chaos did a backflip show.

Joy bounced around with glittered socks,
And tried to hug my inner shocks.

And me? I watched, I laughed, I twirled,
Inside this tiny, teeming world.
They're loud, they're weird—but they're my crowd,
My mind's own party, bright and proud.

3. I Tried to Bribe Time

I met Time sipping herbal tea,
Cross-legged, calm, beneath a tree.
I said, "Hey mate, let's make a deal—
A little tweak, no big ordeal."

I've got a calendar full of flair,
A planner that forgot to care.
What if we skip the boring bits,
Like Monday blues and traffic fits?

I winked and slid a brownie near,
"Come on, old friend, let's bend the year.
Just pause the clock when I'm in flow—
And fast-forward when I stub my toe."

Time smirked and said, "You're quite the case,
Trying to bribe the hands of space.
But though I'm flattered by your charm,
I can't be bought with baked alarm."

I then tried to bribe him with a smile,
Offered laughter stacked in a pile.
"Take my Mondays, have my chores—
Just let me dance a little more."

I also tried a dance, I cracked a joke,
Offered coupons, then bespoke.
A free vacation, extra sleep—
Or one more hour I get to keep.

Time leaned back with timeless flair,
"You're fun, my friend, and self-aware.
But all your tricks, and all your plans—
Still have to pass through my own hands."

"Still," it said, "I'll throw you this—
More joy in now, less fear you'll miss.
If I won't bend or freeze or flee—
Then laugh a little... and let it be."

So now when life feels way too tight,
I smile at Time and say, "Alright."
It doesn't slow or turn around—
But somehow... I feel safe and sound.

4. Can You Trust It?

The trees grow wild by mountain streams,
No gardener tends their leafy dreams.
Yet roots run deep and branches sway,
As if some hand still clears their way.

The sparrow sings with empty hands,
No harvest stored, no shifting plans.
Yet every dawn, it finds its bread—
A silent promise gently fed.

The rivers run, the seasons turn,
The stars arrive with steady burn.
Who lights the moon? Who guards the sun?
And still, we fear we walk alone.

The lion hunts, the lilies bloom,
No calendar, no office room.
No task list carved, no grand design,
Yet all unfolds in perfect time.

But here we stand with worried eyes,
Demanding proof from silent skies.
We seek control, yet barely see
The peace that comes with "let it be."

What if you knew you're not alone,
That something moves beneath the stone?
A voice you've silenced just might say,
"You're safe, you're seen, come what may."

But ego builds its mighty wall,
It needs to win, to grasp it all.
And faith, that bird with broken wing,
Still waits to rise, still longs to sing.

So, ask yourself, when storms begin:
Can you let go, and still lean in?
Can you believe when plans fall through
That love unseen still carries you?

Just like a child in mother's arm,
Held not by proof but by the calm.
The universe aligns when you begin—
Because it's **you** without the doubt within.

5. Not Yet, But Not Never

Inside a place all soft and tight,
Two tiny twins grew in the night.
They kicked and rolled, they dreamed and played,
In warmth and dark, they gently stayed.

"I think there's more," the first one said,
"A world beyond this little bed.
Where light exists and people run,
And skies are blue beneath the sun."

The second sighed, "That sounds too wild!
You speak like some excited child.
There's nothing more—this here is all.
Just floating quiet, a cozy wall."

"But don't you feel that gentle hum?
Like someone's heart, a steady drum?
I think it's her—the one they call
The Mother, holding through it all."

"Have you ever seen her face?
Or touched her hand or felt embrace?
She's just a tale, a made-up sound.
There's nothing real beyond this round."

The first one smiled, "You'll see, you'll know—
When it is time, we all must go.
And when we do, the truth will shine,
That someone loved us all this time."

The time then came, the light broke in,
A cry was heard, a breath, a grin.
And as he left that warm cocoon,
He blinked beneath the silver moon.

He met the hands he always knew,
The heart whose beat had pulled him through.
And in her eyes, so wide and kind,
He saw the proof he'd hoped to find.

6. Almost Right

"Live in the moment," they say with a swipe,
Capturing joy, in a quick hashtag type.
But the soul's been whispering, clear and bright,
That this moment is all, it's the infinite light.

"No strings attached," they joke with a grin,
But detachment is freedom, where true peace begins.
Let go of the world, of the ego's tight spin—
For you came alone, and alone you'll win.

"Chase your dreams," they all scream with delight,
But the Gita would say, the dream's in your sight.
You're already whole, you're already right—
Stop chasing the world, just rest in your light.

Self-love, they say, is their new-found creed,
But the sages have known this, the truth that you need.
The love that you seek, it's not based on greed—
It's the love for the soul, the love you must feed.

"You do you," they shout, in their own little song,
But self-awareness is where they belong.
The more you let go, the more you are strong—
The universe sings, its voice pure and long.

So yes, Gen Z, you're on the right track,
You're speaking the truths that the ancients unpacked.
But listen a little deeper, and you'll see the knack—
The words are the same, but the meaning is back.

7. Time Folded Like a Paper Sheet

One quiet night, the world stood still,
The stars bent low beyond the hill.
Time folded like a paper sheet,
And there I stood — with my own feet.

She looked like me, but seemed so wise,
With calm and fire behind her eyes.
She smiled like she had known it all —
My every rise, my every fall.

"I've walked the roads you've yet to take,
I've felt the cracks, I've seen you break.
But every wound you'll ever earn
Will teach your stubborn soul to learn."

"You chase the light, but fear the dark,
You hide your fire, ignore your spark.
But someday soon, you'll rise so tall,
You'll thank the pain that made you fall."

She held my hand and showed me dreams
That once got lost in silent screams.
She told me, "You are not too late,
The stars still shift — you choose your fate."

Then just like that, she disappeared,
And all the sounds of time appeared.
The wind returned, the sky turned grey,
But something new had come to stay.

A softer heart, a braver mind,
A little more of me to find.
For once, time opened up its shell,
And let me meet my future self.

8. The Mirage of More

He built his throne on golden sand,
With gems that glowed at his command.
Yet deep within, his soul ran dry—
A desert hid beneath the sky.

Ravana rose with mighty grace,
Ten heads, ten minds — one fateful chase.
He conquered all, yet failed to see,
That power blinds when hearts aren't free.

They worship wealth, forget the cost,
In chasing 'more', what all is lost.
A palace rings, but feels alone,
If love departs and pride is sown.

Abundance isn't coins or stone,
Its hands held tight when winds have blown.
Its laughter shared without a price,
A simple meal, a heart made nice.

Some call it growth to rise and reign,
But not all rise removes the chain.
True wealth is peace that doesn't shake,
When storms arrive or empires break.

For even kings with realms so vast,
Can fall for ghosts from lifetimes past.
Abundance lives where kindness stays,
Not just in gold or garlanded praise.

So, weigh your life not by your chest,
But who still stays when you have less.
A mind at ease, a soul that's kind
That's where the richest treasures bind.

9. The First Home I Ever Knew

Before I knew the world outside,
I lived beneath your heart, and cried—
Not out of grief, but quiet grace,
A soul in waiting, tied to place.

No lullaby could match the tone
Of heartbeat hums I called my own—
They cradled me in sacred sound,
Where love, not language, wrapped me 'round.

You knew my needs before my name,
You warmed my fears before they came—
No bond I've known has held that fire,
That soft, unspoken, fierce empire.

When others walked away too soon,
You stayed beneath my midnight moon—
A constant star I cannot chart,
Yet feel forever in my heart.

You broke to build, you bled to give,
You chose to dim so I could live—
And though the world may crown a king,
It's mothers who give angels wing.

Your silence taught, your touch would preach,
What books and sermons couldn't reach—
No mirror shows me more of me
Than eyes that once saw who I'd be.

Through time's long march, and seasons grey,
Your love has never lost its way—
It's not just flesh and bone that blend,
But soul to soul, where time won't end.

And should I ever lose my way,
Or fail to find the words to pray—
I'll hear your hum, that hidden chord,
The first and final voice I've stored.

So let the poets praise their muse,
And lovers sing of wins and bruise
But I have known a holier part
The hand that shaped my beating heart.

**My truth, my home, my silent cover
You were, you are... my dearest mother.**

15. The Quiet Between the War

He stood with doubt, his bow unstrung,
While war drums roared and arrows sung.
But truth arrives not loud, but low—
A whisper where the wise ones go.

"Do not mistake the world for you,
Nor blur the false and what is true.
Your role is action, not the prize;
Let stillness bloom behind your eyes."

The soul is not this weary frame,
Nor praise, nor blame, nor loss, nor name.
The doer fades, the deed remains,
Beyond both triumphs and their chains.

Plant seeds, but let the fruit be free
Release what you're not meant to see.
To work in peace, detached, aware
Is worship hidden in the air.

A sword of love, a shield of grace,
A calm that storms cannot erase.
To give your all, then walk away
That is the yogi's silent way.

He raised his bow—not for the fight,
But as a beacon held to light.
For in the chaos, loud and wide,
He found the war was fought inside.

And there he stood, with eyes now clear,
No longer ruled by doubt or fear.
For Krishna drove the chariot's way—
And *dharma* dawned with each new day.

11. A Discussion Too Long

Is it right or is it wrong?
Alas! That is a discussion too long.
Lie to steal, a punishment you reap
yet lying to save, is a chivalrous deed.

The beggar on the street, stole a treat,
when asked by the merchant, he didn't agree.
Oh! He lied to steal, what a creep!
He looked away and shuffled his feet.

This lie by the tramp, the merchant didn't buy
followed him to his house; he wanted to spy.
There he saw a bed made of hay,
on which the beggar's sick wife lay.

Well, the tramp had the treat indeed,
but not for him, t'was the wife he wanted to feed.
A tear trickled down the merchant's eye,
He sighed and watched the world pass by.

12. It's Nothing But The...

For some the God for some the devil,
For some a boon for some a trouble,
It shapes our world, both kind and cruel,
For some it's wise, for some a fool.

Feeble in memory just as a bubble,
For some complicated and for some subtle,
It dances in shadows, both near and far,
A fleeting wisp or a guiding star.

Ambition, direction, perfection, creation,
Fiction for some for others conviction,
It fuels the fire, both wild and wide,
A silent storm we hold inside.

For some, hatred—for some, affection,
A mind's design in strange direction.
Each thread a part of deeper revealing,
A maze of truth in tender peelings.

How? is a matter of Godly dealing.
A silent spark beyond all feeling.
It's all stored in the bubble we draw,
It's nothing but the dream we saw!

13. The Gaze That Changed the Sky

I looked at stars, they seemed to glow,
Then dimmed a bit, then let me know.
They changed a little, just for me —
As if they knew I came to see.

The leaves were still, then danced along,
The breeze began to hum a song.
It wasn't there a breath ago,
But showed up just to let me know.

The world was quiet, calm, and still,
And then it moved to match my will.
It never spoke a word out loud,
But somehow changed when I was proud.

The river curved where once it stayed,
The sky grew light, then slowly grayed.
The clouds would shift, the colors blend,
As if they knew how I'd pretend.

My silence made the shadows shake,
A blink, and then the lines would break.
What once was real had turned around —
It danced, it paused, it made no sound.

I laughed, and saw the flowers bloom,
I frowned; they vanished from the room.
The echo of my every thought,
Was stitched in things I never bought.

So now I smile and hold my gaze,
At skies, at trees, at gentle rays.
For what I see is shaped and stirred,
By every thought, and dream, and word.

And maybe all I hoped was true —
The world became because I *knew*.
It watched me too, with quiet grace...
And mirrored back my inner space.

PART II

THE SOUL IN FRICTION

14. A Conversation I Had with the Wind

One night I ventured into the dark,
to take a stroll in a lonely park.
My hair gushed by the air, like a string it had twinned
And then O' clock began my conversation with the wind!

"O Wind! You restless thread;
You've kissed the cliffs and mountains ahead
You've danced where the oceans met
And rested where the sun has set

I believe you have seen it all
From the dreary cave to the waterfall
Do you recall the streets I left?
When I was young, fragile and not as deft?

I envy you how you're versatile
Without fretting travel every mile
Freedom to be whatever you want
Nobody to judge or daunt"

"You fool" she said, "don't be naive"
"I can only exist, can't thrive
I carry storms I cannot choose,
And wander lands I'll always lose."

The wind then danced around my cheek
A hush, a whistle, soft and meek
You envy flight but miss the song
Of staying still, where you belong

And as her echo thinned and thinned,
I wept - a conversation I had with the Wind!

15. The Code Behind the Thoughts

A whisper forms before it speaks,
A flicker starts before it peaks.
The brain rewrites without a pen,
Old ghosts dissolve and breathe again.

A word is more than sound or air,
It plants a world; it builds a stair.
Say "light," and see the tunnel bloom
Say "lost," and shape yourself a tomb.

The past's not stone—it's soft, its clay,
Beliefs bend slowly, then obey.
The mind will march where words have led,
A single shift rewires the thread.

"I can," you say—and neurons spark.
A map redraws inside the dark.
Not magic, no—but near enough,
When thoughts turn grit to golden stuff.

Each sentence forms a silent key,
Unlocking who you choose to be.
You change your script, you change your skies
New doors appear where endings lie.

Not trick, nor trance, but tuning in,
To catch the glitch beneath the grin.
And there—beneath your every "why"—
The code rewrites, and fears comply.

16. The Eavesdropping Walls?

What if these walls could hear my sighs,
The muffled thoughts that fill the skies?
What if they knew each whispered plea,
Each tear that fell, so silently?

What if they saw each quiet move,
The moments when I find my groove?
The dance of dreams within my mind,
The secrets that I keep confined.

What if these walls could feel the strain,
The weight of loss, the touch of pain?
Could they sense my heart's silent cry,
Longing for peace, a way to fly?

They've seen it all, from dawn to dusk,
The laughter shared, the bonds we trust.
From joy to sorrow, love's sweet call,
These walls have witnessed one and all.

They've felt the warmth of hands that pray,
The quiet steps when night meets day.
In every crack and faded hue,
The stories of me and you.

So, if you pass these walls so still,
Know they have felt the fire, the chill.
And in their silence, they will keep,
The promises we've sworn to seek.

17. Where Chaos Finds Retreat

He walks where stars forget to shine,
In wrathful grace, both cruel and kind.
The skies recite His fiercest name,
The cosmos bows before His flame.

With ashes smeared and eyes ablaze,
He spins the end in Shiva's gaze.
His matted locks hold time and tide,
The Ganga flows where storms abide.

He roars, the mountains lose their might,
He breathes, and day dissolves to night.
The serpent coil around His throat,
Where death itself forgets to float.

No crown He wears, no throne He needs,
The universe through Him proceeds.
A drumbeat births the yugas' tale,
And when He dances — worlds turn pale.

He wears the moon upon His brow,
Yet wields destruction in His vow.
One glance, and demons cease to be,
He sips the poison, calmly, free.

The fire bends to touch His feet,
He is where chaos finds retreat.
The boldest gods in silence bow,
For none match Shiva's silent vow.

I seek no more a path well-planned,
I'd rather walk where He might stand.
For what is fear when He is near?
Om Namah Shivaya — loud and clear.

18. Talking to the Moon

I talk to the moon when the night turns slow,
Like he's an old friend from lifetimes ago.
He listens in silver, all patient and wide,
Holding the secrets that lovers can't hide.

He's played every role in romance's play—
A mirror, a witness, a guide on the way.
Poets and dreamers have carved him in ink,
Yet never quite grasped what he truly must think.

He's watched first glances and kisses that burn,
And hearts that broke with no promise to return.
He's danced on windows of stories undone,
And whispered in grief, "You're not the only one."

He's flattered for years, with the same old line:
"Your face is the moon"—oh, that age-old sign!
Yet never complains, just quietly beams,
Feeding the midnight with lovers' old dreams.

I ask him at times if he's ever been kissed,
Or if he just glows from the warmth he has missed.
He chuckles in clouds, keeps wearing his grace,
Like a groom always left at the aisle in space.

He knows all the names one has tried to forget,
He hums every song they still regret.
He floats in the ache of "could have been,"
And drapes it in silver so it won't be seen.

But tonight, I won't cry, I won't even swoon—
I'll just raise a toast to my meddlesome moon.
Not a god, not a ghost, just love's little spy,
Smuggling heartache across the sky.

So, here's to the moon, the silent buffoon,
Drifting through poems and meddling too soon.
I'll tell him my tales, till the dawn peeks through—
For if I must ache, I'll ache with a view.

19. What is Fear?

Fear is a shadow, lingering near,
A whisper that doubts the light we hold dear.
It's the absence of faith, a tremor of mind,
A crack in the strength we're yet to find.

Why fear the spider, so small, so mild,
When its purpose is harmless, just nature's wild?
It's the mind that builds monsters from thin air,
Faith, the key, to banish despair.

In the face of unknown, we freeze and we wait,
As if the future is sealed by some fate.
But when we trust, when we step and we leap,
Fear dissolves, and courage wakes from its sleep.

Faith is the force that quells the storm,
A light in the dark, keeping us warm.
For every fear that claws at the soul,
Faith is the strength that makes us whole.

Fear is but a lesson, a test on our way,
It fades when we trust in the light of the day.
So what is fear, but a fleeting illusion,
Replaced by the faith that sparks our conclusion.

20. Love Thyself

I used to seek a voice outside my own,
A whisper, a nod, to make me feel known.
But now I stand, without needing the crowd,
In my own embrace, my spirit is loud.

I once searched for love in places unknown,
Yet found it within, where seeds were sown.
I've learned to cherish the person I see,
A soul that's been loving, a heart that's free.

No longer bound by their judgment or gaze,
I've found my own rhythm, my own pace.
Each scar on my skin tells a story untold,
Of resilience, of strength, of being bold.

I don't need a crown to say I am crowned,
For in my own heart, my worth is profound.
I've learned to nurture the love I once sought,
For I am the treasure I had always thought.

I've learned to embrace the truth I once hid,
To love myself fully, with nothing to forbid.
In my reflection, I now see the light,
A being of power, both tender and bright.

With every step forward, I claim what's mine,
The courage to shine, to let my soul align.
No longer afraid of the road that's ahead,
I walk it with love, with no fear or dread.

The mirror now shows not just a face,
But a soul that's grown, with its own grace.
Self-love, a journey that's deeply profound,
A sacred space where my worth is found.

21. The Gut Knows It First...

It's not the mind that rings the bell,
Nor heart that always dares to tell.
Before the facts, before the cue
A whisper rises straight from you.

A twist, a turn, a sudden chill,
A pause when all else pushes will.
No logic here, no chart, no plan,
Just quiet signs beneath the scan.

You feel it in the shift of air,
In heavy silence hanging there.
A jolt before the words are said
A signal flaring in your head.

They'll say it's nerves, a passing phase,
Dismiss the shiver as a craze.
But you have known this pulse before
The gut that knocks behind the door.

It's ancient, raw, not taught in schools,
It speaks in breaks, in bends, in rules.
The truth arrives without a sound,
And tells you, *"Leave"* or *"Stay your ground."*

So, trust the pull you can't explain,
The lurch beneath your skin and brain.
The body doesn't need a script
It knows the path; it knows the crypt.

22. The Shadows in the Mirror

He was gentle once, with dreams held tight,
A boy who danced in morning light.
His eyes would sparkle at the rain,
He found deep joy in little gain.

He spoke with kindness, soft and slow,
And helped the flowers learn to grow.
But slowly came a different sound
A louder crowd, more harsh, less bound.

They laughed at things he held as dear,
Dismissed his truth, they mocked his fear.
He stayed at first, just for a while,
But soon he wore their crooked smile.

They taught him strength was cold and loud,
To bow to none and please the crowd.
That kindness was a losing game,
And silence brought no pride or fame.

His voice grew sharp, his laughter thin,
He wore the world like borrowed skin.
The songs he loved, he left behind,
Replaced by noise and restless mind.

But deep inside, the echo stayed,
Of who he was before he strayed.
The stars he watched, the dreams he drew
Still whispered truths he once knew.

So, choose your circle with deep care,
For every soul can dim or flare.
You mirror those you linger near
Their light, their dark, their love, their fear.

23. Mirror Mirror on the Wall

Mirror Mirror on the wall,
Who is the happiest of us all?
You are showing me someone I can't recall,
You are forcing my brain to exercise a haul.

Yet the mirror had the courage,
It still did not change the image,
Said "The happiest person is thy,
But I don't know why you deny?"

Mirror Mirror, on the wall,
You are not showing me, for what I call;
Me, the happiest person ever?
Oh! No, not at all

The mirror, firm on its view,
Even I knew what I had to do
Could take no more such torment,
I was ready to put forth some argument.

I am not the strongest person, you see,
How can you still believe it's me?
"You asked for the happiest person, master
Not a competitor for Bruce Lee!"

I don't earn as much, not very wealthy,
How can you still believe it's me?
"You asked for the happiest person, master,
Not a CEO of a top MNC!"

I am not the most intelligent of all,
How can you still believe it's me?
"You asked for the happiest person master,
Not for the finder of gravity!"

I am not the most Handsome man on Earth
How can you still believe it's me?
"You asked for the happiest person, master
Not for Mr. Universe! You see..."

I possess none of what makes someone happy,
How dare you claim that it's me!
"It's not me who is the sinner master,
It's you who has defined happiness wrongly.

Happiness was never confined in the physical realm,
It was always your core reality.

An abstract state of being,
How did you think you'd be able to materially see?"

Mirror Mirror on the wall
What you show, now I recall.
It's me who is the happiest of all,
Mirror Mirror on the wall...

24. Bappa Logged In

In a world where hearts once prayed in still,
Now tap screens and switch with digital will.
Gone are the days of the simple, the true,
Now devotion's a click, and it's nothing new.

The soul's journey once took paths so deep,
Now it streams online while the masses sleep.
So, let's imagine, with a wink and a smile,
What if the divine too adapted this style?

He landed not on lotus bloom,
But in a cab with extra room.
The driver said, "Where to, my lord?"
He smiled and flashed a metro card.

With modaks packed in eco-tins,
And AirPods tucked beneath his skins,
He clicked a selfie, tagged the spot —
#BappaIsBack and stirring thought.

He scanned a QR at the gate,
"Temple closed? That's okay, mate."
He streamed his aarti live instead,
And blessed the comments as they read.

He ordered books on Vedic tech,
Then asked Alexa for a Sanskrit deck.
His mouse-shaped Mushak zipped around,
And chased dropped laddoos off the ground.

He strolled through parks with cheerful cheer,
And paused when children drew him near.
They asked him, "Will you play a bit?"
He laughed and took the bat to hit.

He stopped to help a tea stall man,
Whose fuse had blown, disrupting plan.
With just one tap, the lights returned —
The kettle sang, the burners burned.

He danced to drums near city square,
With rang and joy and festive flair.
No throne, no crown, no pomp or pause —
Just barefoot grace and grand applause.

So, if you spot a kind old man,
Who hums a tune and lends a hand,

Look close — you might just see that spark,
  Of Bappa walking through your park.

25. The Art of Response v/s Reacting

Neurons fire, a spark, a flinch, a jolt,
Reacting fast, like a fire that'll bolt.
It's pure reflex, a primal urge to act,
Without a thought, just an instinctive pact.

But to respond is a different affair,
A pause, a breath, to handle with care.
The brain's cortex takes its time to decide,
Not just to surge, but to step aside.

Reacting's like a car with no brakes,
Zooming ahead, no room for mistakes.
While responding is steering through the curve,
A calm approach, with wisdom to serve.

So next time you're hit with a sudden blast,
Don't just react, make your response last.
Take a moment to pause, reflect and choose,
In response, you'll find the strength to refuse.

It's not the reflex that defines your stance,
But the mindful moment you take to advance.
In that pause, you hold the key to control,
For reaction may blind, but response frees the soul.

PART III

THE SOUL REMEMBERS ITSELF

26. My Lemonade Theory

When life tossed lemons on my bed,
I sipped the pulp and smiled instead.
Not every sour is meant for pain,
Some drops just dance like summer rain.

I took those lemons, made a toast,
Twirled them around, and loved them most.
A dash of sparkle, just for fun,
And turned the sour into the sun.

They said, "It stings, don't let it stay,"
But zests, I found, don't wash away.
They cling like songs you hum inside,
A gentle proof that you survived.

So now I toast to bitter days,
To quiet storms and twisty ways.
Not all that hurts will leave a scar,
Some just remind you who you are.

And if tomorrow feels too bold,
I'll stir the glass with threads of gold.
The recipe? Still not exact —
But lemons? I've got those stacked.

27. The Power of Now

They taught me time moves straight ahead,
From cradle cries to final bed.
A train of moments, neat and wide
But what if time's a trick, not guide?

What if the past still softly breathes,
Inside the folds of falling leaves?
What if the future's not a place,
But shadows shifting in this space?

The clocks may tick, the dates may change,
But life, it doesn't rearrange.
Each moment sings, both old and new,
As if it always somehow knew.

The hands that reach for "what will be"
Might brush against eternity.
No start, no end, no winding line
Just now, disguised in shape of time.

We chase ahead, we call it fate,
But maybe time just contemplates.
A spiral dance, a mirrored hall,
Where every moment holds it all.

So, pause, dear soul, and breathe it in
The echo's not from where you've been.
The now you hold is rich and deep,
It holds both wakefulness and sleep.

28. Inhale, Exhale, Meditate, Become!

I closed my eyes, the world grew thin,
To journey where the soul begins.
No chanting loud, no yogic feat
Just breath and spine, and a grounded seat.

I sat with breath, both soft and slow,
The world behind began to go.
No clocks, no thoughts, no need to be
Just waves of light that swayed in me.

A hum began beneath my skin,
As if the stars had stirred within.
My spine aligned, the mind grew wide,
And peace came rushing like a tide.

Not joy that jumps or screams aloud,
But one that wears a gentle shroud.
A kind of bliss you cannot chase
It finds you in the stillest place.

My hands were still, but skies would spin,
As if the cosmos breathed me in.
Each heartbeat like a sacred drum,
A call to where all things are one.

This is the space where silence sings,
Where breath unlocks celestial things.
This is the gold behind closed eyes
A portal carved in calm replies.

No scriptures needed, no grand sign,
Just breath and being intertwined.
A silence loud, a hush so deep,
It rocked me gently into sleep.

Yet in that sleep, I was awake,
A truth too vast for thought to fake.
No name, no form, just open sea
And in that sea, I melted *me*.

29. You Are Not the Body, Not Even the Mind...

You're not the flesh that wears the skin,
Nor the pulse that stirs within.
The body's but a fleeting dress—
A vessel lost in time's caress.

You are not thought that fills the air,
Not the dreams that rise and tear.
These fleeting whispers come and go—
But you, the silent, steady flow.

Not the words that speak of you,
Not the choices, false or true.
You're not the doubts, not the fears—
You are the stillness that appears.

The mind may race, the body age,
But you, the witness, never stage.
Beyond the sound, beyond the sight,
You are the boundless, endless light.

The essence vast, the truth you seek,
Lies in the silence, soft and sleek.
Not of form, not of mind,
But the eternal truth, undefined.

30. The Infinite Versions of Me

I am the dreamer, I am the sage,
I am the scholar, I am the wage.
I am the humble, I am the grand,
I am the billion in a golden hand.

I am the scientist, lost in thought,
I am the artist, with colors I've sought.
I am the teacher, I am the thief,
I am the world, beyond belief.

I am the soldier, I am the king,
I am the voice that the silence brings.
I am the poor man, bound by pain,
I am the rich, with nothing to gain.

In every realm, I rise, I fall,
Each version of me hears its call.
Tap the frequency, let it unwind,
The countless me's, in the cosmic mind.

The power's within, it's all in your hands,
Raise your vibrations, and the world understands.
In that stillness, all things align,
The universe answers, when you refine.

31. The Throne Between Breath and Thought

Between the inhale's hush and exhale's sigh,
There sits a space where echoes die.
Not time, not flesh, not fears we brought—
Just the throne between breath and thought.

It is not wide, nor cast in stone,
Yet there the soul is most alone.
No crown, no robe, no kingdom sought,
Still power spills from silent thought.

The mind may churn, the pulse may race,
But stillness holds a sovereign place.
No chant, no prayer, no fire caught—
Just still command from breath to thought.

A realm where voices kneel and fade,
Where even light is self-made shade.
The ego bows, illusions rot—
Before the soul who rules unsought.

No gate to find, no map to seek,
No name for strong, no shield for weak.
Yet enter once, and silence schools—
A mystical pause where the soul rules.

32. The Trialogue of Being

Two brothers born within the same mind,
One seeks the light, the other behind.
Conscious, the elder, awake and aware,
Subconscious, the younger, hidden with care.

The elder brother speaks, loud and clear,
He shapes your actions, your thoughts sincere.
In every choice, he takes the lead,
Guiding your steps with the thoughts you heed.

The younger, silent, beneath the veil,
Holds memories, dreams, the forgotten trail.
A storehouse deep, of all that's been,
The whispers of life, in patterns unseen.

But there's a witness, silent and still,
Beyond both minds, untouched by will.
The soul watches, with patient grace,
Observing the dance, without a trace.

While the brothers argue, pull and sway,
The soul stands still, it doesn't stray.
It knows no time, no joy, no strife,
It's the pure essence of eternal life.

Conscious and subconscious, like night and day,
One leads, the other quietly sways.
But the soul remains, in the center of it all,
The observer, the watcher, the answer to the call.

In this trio, they dance, they blend,
One mind, one soul, no beginning or end.
So, in this creation, a masterpiece we see,
How complex we are, how wondrous we can be.

33. Beyond the Finish Line

What is success, a fleeting prize,
A goal to reach, a dream to rise?
Is it the fame, the gold, the cheer,
Or simply living without fear?

Is it a path, a road well paved,
Or are we shackled, left enslaved?
A moment's glory, a fleeting crown,
Or does it rise when we calm down?

Success is more than what you gain,
More than fortune, more than fame.
It's in the work, the sweat, the tears,
The quiet courage through the years.

Success is found not far away,
But in each choice you make today.
In the quiet peace that fills the soul,
And in the heart that's always whole.

So, ponder this, and ask once more,
Is success a dream or something more?
Is it the end or just the start,
A living question in the heart?

34. The Sugar That Healed

A pill was placed in trembling hands,
No drug inside, no crafted strands.
Yet healing came, like whispered grace,
A quiet shift in time and space.

They said, "This helps," and she believed,
And oh, the change her cells received!
Not chemistry, but trust, not fear,
Brought strength that science can't make clear.

What is this force, this gentle trick,
Where mind alone makes bodies tick?
A ghost of hope, a whispered claim,
That lights the dark without a flame.

The heart believes, and so it mends,
Like broken wings that sky defends.
No magic spell, no doctor's might,
Just inner stars that choose to fight.

For often pain is not just real
It's how we *feel* the things we feel.
And sometimes just a kindly lie,
Can lift a soul too tired to try.

So, call it fake, or call it mind,
But still, it leaves no hurt behind.
The body listens when we trust,
And turns belief to healing dust.

What power lies in thoughts we keep?
A word can wake, a word can sleep.
Perhaps the cure's not in the drug
But how it hugs the soul it hugs.

35. The Quiet Art of Saying Thanks

I've learned that joy wears quiet shoes,
It tiptoes in with morning hues
In sips of chai, in softened skies,
In questions that don't need replies.

Gratitude is not a shout,
It's gentle, steady, deep throughout
It lingers in a shared embrace,
And lights the corners time can't trace.

For laughter born of simple things,
For songs the breeze and sparrow sings—
For books unread, but always near,
For voices that I hold so dear.

I'm grateful for the roads I missed,
For dreams I lost and never kissed
For in that space, I came to see
The art of simply letting be.

For all the meals, both grand and small,
For doors ajar and open hall
For patience wrapped in someone's eyes,
And rain that came to cleanse, not cry.

For friends who stayed, for those who left,
For blessings wrapped in quiet theft—
For failure, not as end, but guide,
That taught me where my truth must hide.

I'm grateful not just when it's clear,
But even when the end seems near
For even then, a truth unfolds:
That grace is shy, but always holds.

So, here's to life in all its hues,
The reds, the golds, the silent blues
To all that bloomed and all that grew
I simply whisper, *thank you, too.*

36. The Playlist of My Soul

A vinyl spins inside my chest, a beat I never chose,
It hums beneath my laughter, fades beneath my lows.
A needle drops on memory, a static spark of grace,
Each echo is a lifetime stitched in rhythm, rhyme, and
bass.

There's jazz in all my second thoughts, a trumpet of
regret,
A saxophone of should-have-beens, still playing in duet.
But every minor chord I feared, turned into major flow,
When silence hit crescendo and refused to let me go.

My joy is the trendy pop, naive and neon-bright,
It dances in my kitchen and keeps me up at night.
But grief is an indie-folk, all strings and stormy skies,
It sings in rainy windows and whispers soft goodbyes.

My courage hums in rock n' roll with boots that scuff the
floor,
It kicks down every closed-off door I never dared before.

And love's a lo-fi lullaby, it lingers when it ends,
A chorus I keep dreaming of, in harmonies with friends.

My anger plays in techno blinks, a strobe of red and
white,
A beat so fast it burns the fuse and blacks out all the
light.
But peace is ambient forest sounds that bloom beyond
control,
A slow and mossy melody that greened the cracks I
stole.

My fears dropped two remixes, one haunted, one divine,
But both dissolved when faith stepped in with steadier
design.
And sometimes I just press rewind on childhood's open
skies,
To play the sound my mother sang when I had sleepy
eyes.

So, if you ever lose your map or feel you're not quite
whole,
Just close your eyes and tune into the playlist of your
soul.
Some songs may ache, some make you dance, some
teach you to let go—

But all were born from truths you lived, in rhythms only you know.

37. A Song Beneath All the Things

The universe hums in a silent tune,
In every dusk and every noon.
A pulse beneath what eyes can't see,
A whispered thread of energy.

The atoms spin in secret ways,
Their hums concealed in cosmic haze.
Our words, our thoughts, our smallest sighs
Are actually frequencies that never die.

A cello's bow, a sparrow's wing,
Even silence has its own ring.
Each moment moves with hidden grace,
A ripple in the boundless space.

The stars converse in ancient codes,
Through light that dances, then explodes.
The moonlight too, it sings its part,
A lullaby to every heart.

The radio crackles, strings are strung,
In every beat, a song is sung.
The wind, the sea, the trembling leaf—
All echo tones beyond belief.

From mountain peaks to the ocean floor,
Vibrations knock on every door.
Even our tears, both joy and ache,
Send waves across the soul's own lake.

A voice can soothe, a tone can scar,
We vibrate with just who we are.
Each laugh, each gasp, each spoken truth,
Builds frequencies since tender youth.

The light you see, the sound you hear,
All dance on waves both far and near.
We're made of motion, breath, and flame
No single cell is still or tame.

And so, we live, and so we feel,
In every wound, the power to heal.
A world composed of unseen strings,
A song beneath all living things.

Tune in, and you might just perceive
The ways our pulses interweave.

A symphony that has no end
Where every soul and thought transcend.

PART IV

THE SOUL IN FLIGHT

38. The Soul's Weight on a Feather Scale

They say the soul is light as air,
Yet mine feels heavy, stripped and bare.
If judged not by a steel-built tale,
Then place it on a feather's scale.

A single plume, so soft, so still,
Could test the depth of human will.
Not mass, but meaning, truth, and grace—
The unseen weight our hearts embrace.

Would kindness tip the balance more
Than battles I have fought before?
Would mercy float or sink like lead,
When weighed beside the tears I've shed?

I wonder if my quiet ache
Would make that feather bend or break.
Would laughter lift, would rage descend,
Would silence weigh more than the end?

No gold, no sin, no grand acclaim,
No etched-in-stone, immortal name—
Just whispers that I leave behind,
The weightless thoughts I gift to time.

And when I reach the final gate,
With nothing left to complicate—
I pray my soul will rise, not fail,
Upon that trembling feather's scale.

39. The Spine of Chakras: A Journey Within

At **Mūlādhāra**, red and deep,
The root of trust begins to sleep.
But once it stirs, the ground it holds
Is steadier than myth foretold.

Svādhiṣṭhāna sways in hues of flame,
Desire and flow without a name.
Here, passion forms a molten stream,
The womb of art, the source of dream.

Bright gold, the **Maṇipūra** flame,
Ignites the will, proclaims your name.
Not power's roar, but quiet might—
The sovereign sun that fuels the fight.

Anāhata, soft and green,
A space where joy and ache convene.
It beats for love, it sings, it grieves—
It teaches how the soul believes.

At **Viśuddha**, blue and pure,
The voice becomes a sacred cure.
No mask remains, no silence hides—
The soul at last in truth abides.

Then opens **Ājñā**, twilight's eye,
The brow that sees beyond the sky.
Illusion lifts, the false unbinds—
A mirror lit with ancient minds.

And at the crown, where stars unfold,
Sahasrāra spins in threads of gold.
No self remains, no bounds, no roles—
Just pure awareness, stitching souls.

Each wheel aligned, a thread unspun,
A symphony from root to sun.
The body sings in colored scrolls,
Seven lights, seven gates, seven souls.

So, if you ache and seek and strive,
These **chakras** hum, and keep you alive.
The spine's not bone, but cosmic beams—
A ladder etched in ancient dreams.

40. The Cosmic Vision: A Revelation Beyond Time

Behold the realm where time unbends,
Beyond the stars where space ascends.
A form that spans the vast unknown,
Infinite, where all things are sown.

In every breath, the cosmos stirs,
The universe in endless whirs.
A single flame, yet burning bright,
The sacred glow of endless light.

Not bound by earth, nor sky, nor sea,
A vision vast, a mystery.
The soul, it weeps with knowing eyes,
To glimpse the truth where spirit flies.

In every atom, life is spun,
In every shadow, light begun.
The cosmic dance, a swirling tide,
Where time and space no longer hide.

I stand beyond, yet within me all,
The stars, the moon, the rise, the fall.
A being born, yet death shall cease—
In me resides eternal peace.

The form of all that's felt, and more,
Where life and death have met before.
A world unknown, where none can rule,
A mystic realm, the soul's true school.

A mystical pause where all unrolls,
Where time and space begin to fold.
The boundless truth, the endless gaze,
The soul in flight through cosmic maze.

41. The Way Beyond Mine

I whispered dreams into the night,
With candles lit and heart held tight.
The stars, I thought, had heard my plea,
The skies would bend their will for me.

I wrote the wish in golden ink,
I shaped it whole; I didn't blink.
Each breath a chant, each step aligned,
Each sign I took as heaven's sign.

But when the day of truth had dawned,
The dream I'd fed was somehow gone.
The door I knocked on didn't budge,
The winds moved past; they wouldn't nudge.

It hurt—I won't pretend it didn't.
My soul was cracked, though never hidden.
But in that crack, the light came through,
A whisper said, *"I'm saving you."*

I don't know what lies up ahead,
But not all paths are meant to tread.
And though it broke me, still I say
It's not *my* way; it's the *best* way.

I trust the script I cannot see,
The higher mind that governs me.
What didn't bloom was not a loss
It cleared the way for grander cause.

So here I stand, not less but more,
Not begging fate, not keeping score.
For I believe—yes, still I do
The universe is always guiding true.

42. Waves of Creation

Mind: I am the creator, the spark of thought,
What I envision, I've surely got.
My waves of electricity, sharp and clear,
Manifest worlds from what I hold dear.

Heart: Ah, but dear Mind, you often forget,
It's my emotions that make things set.
It's the pull of feeling, deep and true,
That gives your thoughts the power to come through.

Mind: But without me, how would you know what to
feel?
Thoughts shape the dream, give it form, make it real.
I light the path, I draw the line,
Without my vision, what would you define?

Heart: Yet, without me, your thoughts remain still,
A spark without flame, a dream without will.
Emotion fuels the thought's flight,
Without it, your vision's lost in the night.

Mind: So, what you're saying, is that we both play a
part?
It's the combination that truly sparks the start?
Together, we create, with waves intertwined,
The power of the universe, from thought and heart
combined?

Heart: Yes, indeed, for without both we're blind,
Like electromagnetic waves, we're perfectly aligned.
Thought and emotion, in sync and free,
That's when we manifest reality.

Mind: So, together we create, with a rhythm so fine,
Thoughts and emotions, in perfect design.
In waves we move, in sync we stand,
Manifesting the world with the power in hand.

Heart: Indeed, my friend, now we both can see,
The universe responds when we both agree.
Together, we're strong, and together we'll grow,
With every thought and feeling we sow.

43. I Speak to Him Every Night

I speak to him every night...
But you won't ever catch a sight.
Is he the atrocious monster under my bed?
Or is he a wiggly imaginary friend?

I speak to him every night...
His words, they awaken the inner me just right.
His embrace is one everyone hopes they felt
And infinite love is the only language with which it is to
be dealt.

Its him who has been with me through it all
Toasted to my success and lifted me upon my fall.
He has wiped my tears and widened my grin
He ensured circumstances so I'd never stretch myself too
thin.

He watches my every move
Sets up the forthcoming groove.

As long as I'm in touch with him
Nothing at all can make my life dim.

It's still a mystery if he's in mind or I am in his,
He's my guiding light, all I know is this,
Because I speak to him every night...
It's the UNIVERSE, Oh! my chivalrous knight!!

44. I Am Worthy as I Am!

Whether I rise or whether I fall,
Whether I stand or barely crawl,
Through every doubt and exam,
I am worthy as I am.

Whether I work or take a break,
Whether I mend or sometimes ache,
With every silence and telegram,
I am worthy as I am.

Whether I'm loud or gently shy,
Whether I chase or let things fly,
In storm or in calm,
I am worthy as I am.

Whether I'm curvy, thin, or tall,
Whether I stumble or stand through all,
With every scar and glam,
I am worthy as I am.

Whether I'm praised or left unseen,
Whether I'm messy or pristine,
In chaos or in program,
I am worthy as I am.

Whether I'm fierce or softly spoken,
Whole inside or slightly broken,
With every part and diagram,
I am worthy as I am.

Whether I'm scientist or a singer,
Or a technician, or a dreamer,
Beyond each badge or sham,
I am worthy as I am.

Whether I fit or don't belong,
Whether I'm right or sometimes wrong,
In weakness or in plan,
I am worthy as I am.

Whether I bloom or just survive,
Whether I rest or fiercely strive,
In every breath and jam,
I am worthy as I am.

45. The Aura

Invisible whispers that swirl around,
A field of energy, not bound to the ground.
A glow from within, though unseen by sight,
It pulses and hums, soft as the night.

It moves through the body, from head to toe,
A current of life, gentle yet bold.
It speaks in colors, in hues that arise,
A silent language, beneath the skies.

It dances in rhythm with each breath we take,
In stillness or motion, it never will break.
It carries our thoughts, our fears, and our joy,
A cosmic embrace that none can destroy.

Like sunlight that filters through leaves on a tree,
Our aura reflects what the heart longs to be.
A connection, unseen, to all that we know,
A beacon that lights us wherever we go.

The science may measure, the spirit may feel,
But the aura is truth, it's pure and real.
A silent connection, beyond what we know,
It whispers our essence wherever we go.

46. The Memory Within Me

My body speaks in silent codes,
In breathless pause and secret modes.
A gesture flows I've never known,
Yet feels as if it's all my own.

I smile at scents from lifetimes past,
Like jasmine blooms that couldn't last.
My fingers dance on notes unseen,
To music from a different screen.

A glance, a step, a sudden thrill,
Not learned by thought, but deeper still.
The grace I show, the calm I keep,
Are borrowed gifts my cells still sleep.

No tale was told, no book was read,
Yet I recall what once was said.
Like wisdom etched in every pore,
Of all who came and loved before.

Not pain, but light is what I hold,
In stories written, soft and bold.
No sorrow here, just echoes bright,
That guide me with their gentle light.

I am not just a tale of now,
But of the when, the where, the how.
And every cell, in silent cheer,
Keeps every joy I hold most dear.

47. Forms of Love

The whisper of breath on a newborn's face,
A mother's tears in her child's embrace.
The warmth that floods without a name,
Yet burns the soul like sacred flame.

The hands you hold in skies or sand,
That lift you up, that understand.
A silent nod, a knowing smile
Love walks with us each fragile mile.

The artist bows to what he drew,
A world once dreamt now breaking through.
No words exchanged, no need to speak,
Yet love stands tall in brush and streak.

The ragged boy with eyes so bright,
Who grins when gifted one sweet bite.
The joy that needs no wealth or fame
Just kindness sparked into a flame.

The faith Meera poured in song and skin,
For love not bound by loss or sin.
She drank her pain and still she danced,
Each step a prayer, each breath entranced.

The sister's scold, the father's sigh,
The friend who stays when you just cry.
The dog that waits by midnight's gate,
Still wagging, still hoping — still love, innate.

The lover's touch, the partner's vow,
The storm they brave, the peace they plough.
But greater still is love unseen
In tiny acts, in in-betweens.

Not all love wears the same disguise,
Some rise as tears in quiet eyes.
And some are loud, like skies above...
Yet each a mirror — *forms of love.*

48. The Stardust in Our Veins

They say the stars are far and cold,
But ancient skies have truths they hold.
Not magic spells or crystal shows—
Just patterns time and cosmos chose.

The moon tugs tides upon the sea,
Why not the tides inside of me?
If gravity can shape the shore,
Couldn't it shape a little more?

Each orbit, tilt, and stellar dance,
Aligns not fate, but circumstance.
Not puppeteers, but cosmic cues
A nudge, a whisper in our shoes.

Nakshatras etched in Vedic lines,
Mapped meaning to the moon's designs.
Saturn's gaze, a patient test,
Saade Saati: a soul's unrest.

Sun signs speak in metaphors
Of tempered hearts or raging wars.
A Leo roars, a Virgo schemes,
Yet we are more than charted themes.

It's not the stars that bind our path,
But how we read their aftermath.
For science, too, once looked above,
To trace its roots and question love.

So, scoff not at the sky's old chart,
It's less about the fate, than art.
A mirror held in stellar light,
To help us choose what's wrong or right.

And when you feel the world misalign,
Perhaps it's just the planets' sign.
Not control—but conversation—
Between the soul and constellations.

49. The Fourfold Whisper: The Ho'oponopono Prayer

Thank you, for the moments unseen,
For the spaces between, where love has been.
For the lessons disguised in pain,
And for the hearts that heal again.

Sorry, for the wounds that still linger,
For the moments I didn't notice your finger,
Pointing the way, leading me right,
But I missed the call in my blind sight.

Please forgive me, for the times I've failed,
When I've held onto guilt and let love be derailed.
For the words unspoken, the chances missed,
For the moments I walked in shadows, not kissed.

I love you, for the beauty you bring,
For the joy in the small things, the song we sing.
For the ties that bind, the souls we share,
For the silence in which our hearts declare.

Thank you, for the healing that starts within,
For the grace to release where we've been.
For the peace that comes when we set it free,
For the trust in what we are meant to be.

Sorry, for the parts I didn't see,
For the hurts I left, not letting them be.
But in this prayer, I release the weight,
I trust in the timing; I trust in fate.

Please forgive me, for the times I've doubted,
When I've been angry, confused, or clouded.
But now I know, I've come to find,
That peace comes when we heal the mind.

I love you, not for what you've done,
But for the journey we've just begun.
For the gift of presence, the bond so true,
And for the sacred space where we renew.

Four sacred lines, soft as dew,
A chant of healing, pure and true.
From isles where waves and silence meet —
Ho'oponopono: A prayer, to cleanse, to love, complete.

50. The Soul's Ascent to the Five Gates

I. Earth

I knelt where silence touched the ground,
And felt the world without a sound.
The roots below, the skies above
All whispered back in wordless love.

I walked on dust, but felt it sing,
Of every birth and buried king.
It taught me strength that doesn't shout—
But grows within, then ripples out.

II. Water

Through mirrored streams, I dared to tread,
Where sorrow sleeps and truths are said.
The tides held secrets, soft and deep,
Where even grief was lulled to sleep.

I drank from wells that knew my name,
Each ripple rising, none the same.

And learned that tears, both mine and wide,
Can cleanse the soul they used to hide.

III. Fire

The flames stood tall like guards of light,
Yet welcomed me with no respite.
They licked my lies and scorched my pride,
Till nothing false was left to hide.

I walked through blaze and did not break,
But shed the masks I used to make.
In embered breath and ash's glow,
I found the self I did not know.

IV. Air

A wind arose with voices old,
And turned my thoughts to threads of gold.
It sang of things not seen, but true,
Of dreams that skies alone once knew.

It taught me how to float, to trust,
To leave behind the grip of dust.
And whispered this: "You're not your fear
You are the echo only I hear."

V. Ether

No gate to cross, no path to chart

Just silence blooming in the heart.
The soul became what it had sought,
Not something learned, but something *caught.*

In stillness spun beyond the skies,
Beyond all names the mind can prize
I knew not me, nor time, nor place...
Just light embraced in endless grace.

And then—
The soul returns not burnt, but bare,
A breathless note in holy air.
Not who it was, not what it knew,
But something vast—and something true.